Trees in Fall

BY JENNA LEE GLEISNER

The Child's World®
childsworld.com

Published by The Child's World®
1980 Lookout Drive • Mankato, MN 56003-1705
800-599-READ • www.childsworld.com

Photographs ©: iStockphoto, cover, 1, 8–9, 16–17;
XiXinXing/iStockphoto/Thinkstock, 5; Lijuan Guo/
Shutterstock Images, 6; Shutterstock Images, 10,
12–13, 20; iStockphoto/Thinkstock, 14; Forest Chaput
de Saintonge/iStockphoto, 18–19; Creative-Family/
iStockphoto, 22

Design Element: Shutterstock Images

ISBN 9781503816633
LCCN 2016945651

Printed in the United States of America
PA02323

ABOUT THE AUTHOR

Jenna Lee Gleisner is an author
and editor from Minnesota. Her
favorite thing about fall is the
changing colors.

Contents

Winter Is Coming

It is fall. Leaves cover the ground. They crunch underneath our feet.

Fall is **chilly**. Plants get ready for winter.

Falling Leaves

Leaves change color.

Some turn yellow.

Others turn orange
or red.

NO CAMPS
OR FIRES
Within 1/4 mile
of Road

9

Many trees drop their leaves. This helps trees keep water during winter.

Soon all of the leaves fall. The trees are **bare**.

We **rake** the leaves into piles. We like to play in them!

Some trees do not lose their leaves. **Evergreens** stay green all year long.

Tree Homes

Trees are homes for animals. Animals get ready for winter, too.

Squirrels bring nuts into trees. They live in trees during winter.

Leaf Journal

Collect fall leaves!

Supplies:

leaves

book

paper or notebook

clear crafting glue

pencil

Instructions:

1. Collect leaves that have fallen to the ground. Pick your favorite ones!

2. Put your leaves inside a book. Leave them in the book overnight.

3. Use your crafting glue to paste the leaves into your notebook or journal.

4. If you can, label what kind of tree each leaf came from. You can ask for help to learn about the trees near you.

Glossary

bare — (BAYR) Bare means not covered. In fall, some trees are bare after they lose all of their leaves.

chilly — (CHIL-ee) Chilly means cold. Fall is chilly.

evergreens — (EV-ur-greenz) Evergreens are trees that have green leaves all year long. Evergreens do not lose their leaves.

rake — (RAYK) A rake is a tool that can be used to collect leaves. We rake leaves into piles.

To Learn More

Books

Felix, Rebecca. *What Happens to Leaves in Fall?* Ann Arbor, MI: Cherry Lake Publishing, 2013.

Herrington, Lisa M. *How Do You Know It's Fall?* New York, NY: Children's Press, 2014.

Web Sites

Visit our Web site for links about trees in fall: **childsworld.com/links**

Note to Parents, Teachers, and Librarians: We routinely verify our Web links to make sure they are safe and active sites. So encourage your readers to check them out!

Index

24